Midlife Awakenings

Midlife Awakenings

Discovering the Gifts Life Has Given Us

Barbara Bartocci

AVE MARIA PRESS   Notre Dame, Indiana 46556

International Standard Book Number: 0-87793-659-5

Cover and text design by Brian C. Conley
Printed and bound in the United States of America.

Contents

1

A New Way to See

Overheard conversation:
"Are you looking for inner peace?"
"Well, sure. Isn't everyone?"

In the seminars I present to audiences around the country, I remind people that we live our lives the way we sometimes drive a car. Have you ever "come to" behind the steering wheel and wondered for a panicky moment, "Where am I?" You were driving along such a familiar road that you got "lost in thought" and drove automatically until a traffic signal or a freeway exit "woke you up."

For two-thirds of my life I ran on automatic. My thoughts and emotions soared up and down like a West Virginia highway, seemingly out of my control. Then I reached fifty, and something happened.

Has it happened to you?

In midlife, our focus begins to change, going from the outer to the inner; from acquiring to letting go; from the idea that *big-is-better* to *less-is-more*. We no longer strive for possessions, titles, and power in the same way we did in our twenties and thirties. We've had to accept that some early goals will not be reached. We must find gifts in what life has given us. By the mid-forties, everyone has had a share of joy and tribulation until we realize, finally, that "nobody has it all."

This is the decade when we get in touch with our own mortality. A few contemporaries have probably died. ("Did you hear? Joe collapsed on the golf course! An aneurysm, they say. He was only fifty-two!") Perhaps our parents are gone, or have become abruptly old and needy.

At midlife we may ask, "Is this all there is?" Yet even if we yearn for new creative challenges, we no longer worship fifty-hour work weeks. Instead, we want time to deepen our relationships with family, friends, spouses, and God.

For some, midlife brings uninvited changes—loss of a job or marriage or health—and our task becomes how to find meaning in what we never asked for. For others, life proceeds outwardly as before, but what once satisfied no longer does. Big parties, superficial social acquaintances, even conventional volunteer work may pale. We seek something deeper.

Social scientists tell us that people who feel fulfilled in their older years are those who have found a larger meaning for their lives, and fifty is when many of us start looking. Some seek radically new paths. I've known people who, at fifty, join the Peace Corps or down-scale financially in order to pursue a back-burnered dream. Some leave a dead relationship while others breathe new life into old relationships.

Our midlife is less a time of review and more a time to *re-view*—to see differently. It's our chance to stop living on automatic pilot and instead to start paying attention: to come awake. Is this why so many people begin exploring meditative prayer at midlife? I think so. You can't gulp down God like fast food. Tina Turner, fifty-six, has a special room for Buddhist chant. Former New York governor Mario Cuomo meditates daily and keeps a journal.

Learning to sit in the silence has profoundly changed me. Yet I seldom go immediately into meditation. I need a "warm-up," just as I stretch before physically exercising. My meditative warm-ups come through spiritual reading. Religious scriptures offer a grounding; yet other writers, too, appeal to me—as varied as C. S. Lewis, Henri Nouwen, Emmett Fox, M. Scott Peck, Catherine Marshall, Marianne Williamson, Thomas Merton, and Peace Pilgrim. Sometimes I gain spiritual perspectives from like-minded friends or business colleagues. I write down what they say, putting on paper their insights as well as my own. Often what inspires me most are the words of wounded healers, those who don't claim to have all the answers, but who simply share their experience of the way God's grace has worked in their lives.

This is a book of such personal reflections. Many had their genesis in my own prayer journals, but they include the wisdom of various other people as well. In sharing them with you, I hope to serve as a friendly guide for *your* journey through midlife.

2

A New Way to Pray

If the soul keeps far away
from all discourse in words,
the Spirit of God will come into her.
—*Abba Poeman*, Sayings of the Desert Fathers

Meditative prayer is not new, of course. As long as humans have sought God, they have prayed into silence, listening for the still, small voice within. So we're talking about an old, old way to pray, yet for some of us it is a strikingly new experience. I remember the first time I sat down with the idea of merely sitting in God's presence. I felt so nervous! To slow our minds and simply *be* seems extraordinarily difficult in our action-oriented, noise-driven, time-starved western culture when thoughts tumble from past to future like a basket full of puppies clambering on top of one another.

In his wonderful book, *Beginning to Pray*, Orthodox Archbishop Anthony Bloom writes, "We can pray to God only if we are established in a state of stability and inner peace face to face with God. This releases us from the subjective sense that time is running fast and that we have no time left. The mistake we often make with our inner life is to . . . try to live an inch ahead of ourselves. That is what prevents us from being completely in the present moment [and] that is what we must learn about prayer, to establish ourselves in the present."

Maybe you think, as I once did, that meditation requires a lot of time. The more experienced I become in it, the more I rejoice when I am able to sit for thirty to forty-five minutes; but I've also learned that we can sit in silence for as little as five or ten minutes, and gradually the wriggling puppies in our minds calm down. It does help to pray at the same time and in the same place each day because a regular routine creates a pattern that aids in quieting ourselves.

If praying in the silence is new for you, here is a simple ten-step process for ten-minute meditation.

Ten Simple Steps to Ten-Minute Meditation

1. Sit in a chair, on your bed, or on the floor and keep your spine straight though not uncomfortably stiff.
2. Begin with a passage of inspirational reading. Think about the words you just read. What do they say to you about your own life?
3. As you focus, close your eyes and begin taking long, slow breaths—what I call belly breaths—the kind that

start in your abdomen and fill your lungs. Breathe in through your nostrils and release to the count of five through your slightly-open mouth.

4. Breathe this way three times. You'll notice that your body has relaxed. Breathe normally, but notice your breath as it goes in and out. Our breath is such a physical way of *in-spiring*, yet we take it for granted. Notice it now. In . . . out . . . in . . . out.

5. You may choose to mentally repeat a holy word as you breathe: "Jesus." "Peace." "Praise God." When your thoughts wander from your breath and your holy word (as they will), gently bring them back around. No judgment. Simply notice what happens in your mind the way you watch clouds as they drift across a summer sky.

6. Observe the sensations in your body. Most of the time, we carry our bodies around like briefcases, hardly noticing them. Pay attention now. Do your shoulders ache? Is there tension in your belly or your upper back? Notice the actual sensations, not with a goal of changing them, but simply to be aware.

7. If you hear sounds, listen to the sound vibrations: the soft thud of footsteps in the hall outside, the hum of air-conditioning, a dog's bark. Don't think about what they mean. Simply hear them.

8. Return your attention to your breath. In . . . out. Notice how your chest moves as you breathe. Have your thoughts wandered? It's okay. Gently bring attention back to your breath and your holy word.

9. As your ten minutes end, slowly open your eyes. Murmur this prayer: "Thank you, God."

10. Go on to your daily tasks, whether at work or at home. Some people meditate in the morning and again before going to bed. You may choose to meditate just once a day, but gradually expand the time to twenty minutes.

Meditative prayer works best if you look upon it as a gift of *time* that you are giving to God rather than as a process meant to gratify you. Don't hunger for results. Simply experience whatever comes. As you learn to focus your thinking for ten minutes, you'll become more conscious of your thoughts at other times too. You'll start to live more often in the present moment, which is actually all we have. It's when we learn to appreciate *this* moment, without indulging in past regrets or future worries, that we discover the elusive gift of inner peace. This is what the journey past fifty is all about.

Don't stop with meditative prayer. Let your reading lead you into the silence; then let silent prayer open you outward to holy, apostolic action. I've heard it described as God's two-step dance: from prayer to holy action; from action back to prayer.

3

A New Way to Be

Let it be, let it be,
Let it be, let it be,
Speaking words of wisdom,
Let it be.
— The Beatles

Most of us try to do something special to mark our fiftieth birthday. I spent mine in a retreat center that sprawls across several acres of Kansas farmland near the Missouri border. For years I'd given myself a weekend there each February as my birthday gift. Sitting with a prayerful community seemed like an idyllic way to look back over the past year and become spiritually centered for the next year.

This time, as I sat on a prayer rug in the rough-hewn chapel, I felt a happy sense that perhaps I had finally *arrived*.

Getting to fifty had been a rough road in so many ways. It included the untimely death of my first husband when I was twenty-nine; the challenge of raising three small children alone; a return to college as an adult student; a late entry into the work world; and a second marriage that brought more problems than solutions. My children's adolescent years had been particularly turbulent.

Now, though, the kids were living on their own; my second husband and I were working on our marriage; my professional work was going well; and I felt a contented sense of being settled. I shifted on the prayer rug, smelling traces of incense and the dry, peculiar odor of old wood. Through the chapel windows, I spied a rabbit, brown against the snow. It disappeared into a grove of bare-limbed trees, leaving its footprints behind. I was struck by how quickly it darted across the pasture and was gone.

Later, remembering the rabbit, it seemed like an omen, for all too soon my contentment vanished, almost as quickly as the rabbit disappeared. While praying in chapel, I could not know that within six months my husband would abruptly leave me to go reinvent his life in the Colorado mountains. No prescient voice foretold the divorce that would physically, financially, and emotionally shatter me. Nor did I realize that out of my pain I would gradually "come awake" to a new sense of vibrant self-acceptance and creativity, and an unexpected delight in my life as a single woman in my fifties.

I smile as I recall my innocent idea that turning fifty marked an arrival. Now I know it's another way station. The journey *past* fifty can be an extraordinary period of spiritual growth and new beginnings, but only if we accept that we *don't* arrive, that life continues to change, often unexpectedly. It is up to us to discover God's answers inside each change.

I'm reminded of this when I travel down highways in the Midwest where I live. The roads are often bordered by broad farmlands, and I'm always struck by the regular upheaval of soil that is necessary for new growth. What enriches soil and makes it fertile is humus, the nutrient-rich remnant of past plantings. The word *humus* springs from the same root word as *humility*. My divorce was a humbling experience. It hurt. It forced me to rethink my expectations for what "should be." But the upheaval brought new sprouts of green.

Of course, as the song says, "It's not easy being green." It was hard to understand this midlife change. I had to fall back on King Solomon's guidance: "Trust in the Lord with all your heart and lean not on your own understanding." So many of life's changes are hard for our rational minds to understand. We endure, or weep, or grit our teeth, but still feel bewildered.

It helped to remember what Ruth, a community member at the retreat house, had said to me years earlier: "When you sit in prayerful silence, even though nothing appears to be happening, grace is at work." Through grace the Word speaks to us with wisdom, and we discover, at life's midpoint, a new way to be.

4

A New Way to Live

When a dragonfly sits, it simply sits,
not focused on future flights,
past adventures, or an encounter with another
*   dragonfly.*
Meditation is what sitting is to a dragonfly.
—*Edward Hays*, Daily Personal Prayers

May each of these short passages bring you daily words of wisdom and serve as a warm-up for your own silent meditation. After you prayerfully sit in the silence, read the accompanying Holy Action and decide if it's a step you can use in your day.

Acceptance

Once, in the midst of a quarrel, my spouse cried, "Why can't you accept me for who I am?" The anguish of that question immediately stopped me, for isn't that what all of us want—to be loved for who we are? But how can we accept another unless we first accept ourselves? For years, I held myself to an impossible standard of perfection, and if *I* had to be perfect, why, those I loved had to be too. I didn't even accept God as God is, but created my own picture of what I thought God *should* be—a combination of a Fairy Godfather and a Creator who liked to bargain. I wanted God to grant my wishes (I called them prayers) and didn't appreciate a God who allowed into my life the lessons I needed to learn. It's taken me years to understand the wisdom behind something Mother Maria wrote: "The work of love is to see in others the Center [God] as their one reality and then to love them in this reality." I pray today to accept all others in their own reality—including God!

Holy Action: You can love God and your neighbor only to the extent that you love yourself. Look in the mirror, make eye contact with yourself, and say aloud,

"I love myself—both my strengths and my weaknesses."

Notice: Did you believe the words you said aloud? If not, ask the Holy Spirit to aid you in greater self-acceptance. Continue to affirm daily, "I love myself. Not as I will be. Not as I could be. But as *I am*."

Acquiescing

I'm a lot like the apostle Peter before the Holy Spirit transformed him. In John 13, Jesus washes his apostles' feet, and Peter says, "Jesus, Lord, you mustn't," to which Jesus replies, "If I do not wash you, you have no part of me." Immediately Peter says, "Oh, in that case, also wash my hands and head." Dear impulsive Peter, always trying to get just a little bit more—and so quick to tell Jesus what he should do instead of acquiescing to what he does. Am I not like that? How quickly the gifts that come my way are superseded by my desires for more. It reminds me of something I recently read. In 1975, Americans said "the good life" included a car, their own home, a happy marriage, an interesting job, and the ability to send their kids to college. Twenty years later, according to a Roper poll, Americans included in the good life "a lot of money," a color TV, a second car, travel abroad, and a vacation home. Sometimes the more we receive, the greedier we become. When will I learn to keep quiet and simply allow my feet to be washed?

Holy Action: Be alert today to all the gifts that are already in your life. Ask yourself, how much of what you think you *must* have is simply a result of persuasive advertising? What possessions are you holding on to in your basement or attic that you no longer use but are afraid to relinquish because you "might" need them? Give something away that you value but no longer need.

Affirmation

I'm not sure where I saw this, but it's a wonderful affirmation: "I is where I is." Yes! Say it out loud. "I IS WHERE I IS." Wishing I were someplace else won't change a darn thing. Shout it! Sing it! "I IS WHERE I IS." How often we waste precious life energy wishing we could be someplace else. I once heard a sixty-five-year-old acquaintance say, with a touch of melancholy, "I'm just now realizing how little I appreciated my happy times when I was experiencing them." Oh, what a sad realization! Help me find the grace to appreciate right where "I is" today.

Holy Action: For this one day, live in the reality of what is, and accept everything in your life as a gift, both the good and the seemingly bad, recognizing that even apparent problems offer opportunities to grow.

Answers

Thoughts while watching *Jeopardy*, the TV game show. Isn't *Jeopardy* a metaphor for life? The answers are already in place for us; we just have to ask the right questions. In a seminar, Depak Chopra, the physician and author, told a story about the car that picked him up for a ride to the airport. The car was bright yellow, an unusual color, so Dr. Chopra began looking for other glimpses of yellow, asking himself what yellow might mean in his life that day. The car drove past a bright yellow billboard advertising "Celestial Seasonings" tea. Later, on the plane, a man in a yellow jacket approached Dr. Chopra's row of seats and sat down. The yellow-jacketed man turned out to be the executive in the Celestial Seasonings company that Dr. Chopra had wanted to talk to about a project he had in mind. If he hadn't been alert to the color yellow, would Dr. Chopra have spoken to the man? Or, like so many of us when we fly, would he have hunkered down silently behind a paperback book and never glanced at his seatmate? How often do I fail to notice an answer because I'm not asking the question?

Holy Action: Today, be alert to *serendipity*: life's small, unexpected gifts. A phone call from a friend who's been out of touch for several months. Praise from your boss for a job well done. A ray of sunlight that falls across your desk. (Isn't it nice to have sun instead of rain?) Notice the small miracles in the often overlooked details of your day. What answers are they providing? What questions must you ask?

Approval

Jesus was a great psychologist! In the New Testament he says, "You must leave your mother, your father, your sisters, and your brothers to follow me." That seemed like a harsh admonition until one spring day when my kids were teenagers, *I got it.* My mother had phoned, and as so often happened in our conversations, I had hung up with a sense of guilty frustration because we had disagreed over a decision I'd made regarding the kids. *Why do I still let her ring my chimes?* I wondered, and said aloud, "I am not my mother. I'm a different person altogether. I make different choices. *And it's all right.*" I took a deep breath. I had said those words before, but on this spring day, with the redbud tree blooming outside, their truth somehow penetrated. Today's experts use terms like "individuation" to mean we have to separate psychologically from our parents before we can live our own lives. With or without my mother's approval, I realized I was an adult and had to make the choices that seemed right to me. Two thousand years ago in Galilee, when Jesus said, "You must leave your mother and your father," isn't that what he meant?

Holy Action: Write down three positive and three negative messages you heard from your parents when you were young. Ask yourself, "Are the negative messages I heard appropriate to the person I am today?" Restate them in a positive way, reflecting who you are today.

Beauty

More and more women and men are opting for cosmetic surgery. Even in the conservative Midwest, I know someone who invested $50,000 in total body liposuction and another who spent $10,000 for a face-lift at the age of forty. Yet last year, at my Uncle John's funeral, I was struck by the beauty in my four aunts' faces. All are women in their seventies or eighties, and their faces carry the sweet furrows of age. Yet I see in Helen such grace and inner elegance; in Jean, equanimity and the ability to roll with the punches; in Marian, a questioning mind and artistic eye; in Lucille, such warmth and friendliness. Inner spirit transcends youthful skin, something the cosmetologists, with all their creams, lathers, and surgical knives, forget to tell us.

Holy Action: Today, do not waste one moment bemoaning the wrinkles around your eyes or a growing bald spot. Instead, acknowledge something about yourself that is beautiful. Name it. Carry yourself joyfully, with warm appreciation for your natural God-given beauty. May it be your goal not to look younger, but simply to look your best for whatever age you are.

Bookends

My friend Jim reads newspaper obituaries. He's older than I, nearly sixty; still, I was surprised when he told me. "Isn't that morbid?" I said. He laughed. "Well, every now and then, I see a familiar name. And no one sends invitations to funerals, so how else will you know?" My first response, a shiver, reflects our societal view. Americans are so prone to hide from death's reality. Yet aren't birth and death merely bookends? Peace Pilgrim, a saintly woman who spent twenty-eight years walking the highways of this country for peace, wrote, "When you know that you are only wearing the body, which can be destroyed, and that you are the reality which activates the body and cannot be destroyed, how can you be afraid of dying?" If I believe in an existence beyond this life, why not glance at obituaries? Aren't they merely notices of a different birth?

Holy Action: Spend fifteen minutes writing your own obituary. Notice what you put first. Is it your worldly success? Is that really how you want to be remembered? If you died today, will you have fulfilled your unique place in the universal life pattern? Meditate on the question: "What has God given me to do in life?"

Cheerfulness

My daughter Sony brought my grandson Jake to a social gathering. Startled by our noisy conversation, Jake started to cry. "Shhh, Jake. Cheer up," someone soothed. "It takes a lot more energy to be cheerful than to cry," said Sony. It does, doesn't it? It takes energy to do what fulfills you and to stay cheerful in the face of disappointment. A lot of times, it seems easier to give up and bawl. Two hundred years ago, the British satirist Joseph Addison wrote, "I have always preferred cheerfulness to mirth. Mirth is short and transient, cheerfulness fixed and permanent; a habit of mind." Scripture says it more succinctly: A cheerful heart is a good medicine (Prv 17:22). When baby Jake stopped crying and began to smile, the rest of us applauded. Today, I pray for the grace to act from a cheerful perspective, no matter what life brings.

Holy Action: Cheerfulness, unlike happiness, is an attitude rather than a feeling. In his book *The Learned Optimist*, psychologist Martin Seligman, Ph.D., points out that cheerful, optimistic people create better outcomes for themselves. For the next twelve hours, no matter what the circumstances, choose to react in a cheerful manner, even if you have to "fake it 'til you make it." Notice how quickly your feelings catch up with your attitude.

Conflict

My father and my first husband had a lot in common. My dad was a senior Air Force colonel, and John was a young Navy officer who viewed his father-in-law as a mentor. A few years into our marriage, John and I vacationed with my parents. Everyone had a fine time until one evening, as we sat outside, desultorily talking in the August heat, my dad broached the question, "Do military academy graduates make better officers?" John had graduated from Annapolis, but my father had risen through the ranks, and before anyone realized *how* it happened, the discussion grew heated. My dad held some hidden resentments that suddenly emerged. When John tried to change the subject, my dad wouldn't let it go. Finally, I cried, "Daddy, back off or we're leaving." And that's exactly what we did, with me insisting it was up to my dad to call and apologize.

August passed, then September, then October, and my father still hadn't called. Finally, in November, John said, "Barb, I want to invite your folks for Thanksgiving." "But Daddy hasn't apologized," I protested. John replied with three words. "*It doesn't matter*," he said. A few minutes later, I heard him on the telephone: "Colonel, come help me carve our Thanksgiving turkey."

Less than a year later, when my husband's Navy jet crashed off the coast of Vietnam, my dad, in his Air Force dress blues, gave a moving eulogy at John's memorial service. But the words I remember best are the three words that brought them together again: "*It doesn't matter*."

Holy Action: Are you experiencing a personal conflict in your family or with a friend? Can you release the need to be right? Can you turn the other cheek? Can you find the deep, holy place within that will let you say the words, "*It doesn't matter*"? Say them aloud. If the words stick in your throat, write in your journal about what holds you back, and ask for the Holy Spirit's help to let go.

Conformity

Several years ago, stories appeared in the media about an adolescent boy who became so concerned about the homeless that he started raising money to help them. Eventually, this teenager raised thousands of dollars. I thought of him when I read what Fr. Richard Rohr, O.F.M., said about saints. "Saints often faced family and friends who told them to be satisfied with just being good, just obeying the Commandments, just going to church and leading a decent life, just making a living and getting along like everybody else. Saints have to struggle with the temptation just to be good and conform to what is socially acceptable instead of reaching out for holiness." I could picture this boy's parents saying, "Son, just get good grades and don't do drugs. This other—going door to door to raise money for the homeless? Let the government take care of it. You concentrate on school work so you can get into a good college." After all, didn't the family of Jesus try to persuade him to come home to Nazareth and take up his father's trade? We like it when people are good. Especially if they conform. We don't really like it when they get holy. That's why saints make news.

Holy Action: Think of an action you might take that involves some personal risk. You might choose not to laugh at a joke that is offensive or quietly express consternation when a friend or work colleague makes a disparaging remark about a certain ethnic group. Or you might write a letter to the editor and publicly defend an action that is morally right but unpopular. If you see no immediate opportunity, spend a few minutes in prayer affirming the courage you are seeking when the opportunity does arise.

Continuum

Thoughts in the steam room at the gym two weeks after my fiftieth birthday: I am part of a continuum. Others will come after me, as I have come after my forebears. When I die, it will be as if the ocean has lost one drop of water. The ocean itself goes on, just as the force of life will go on. Problems that loom large in my life are merely light swells when viewed from the perspective of eternity. Though I believe in a personal God, a God who is close and available, I need to remember that God sees me as neither in isolation nor at the center. I am a water drop, a tiny part of the whole.

Holy Action: The sense of ego-centered separateness occurs when we judge, criticize, or compare ourselves to others. Today practice "oceanic consciousness" by looking for what connects you to others rather than at what separates you.

Control

Anthony Bloom, the Orthodox archbishop, once told an interviewer, "The only question I ask is, 'What should I do at this particular moment?' I never ask myself what the result of an action will be—that is God's concern. All you can do is be at every single moment as true as you can with all the power in your being—and then leave it to God to use you, even despite yourself." I ponder these words, thinking how much I like to control outcomes. Last year, I got stuck on a steep ski run. "Let your skis go," called the ski instructor. "You'll be at the bottom in three turns." But I clung to where I was, afraid of losing control. Finally, fearfully, I made one turn . . . then another . . . then another . . . and the instructor was right. I reached the bottom. Without falling! Whatever I'm doing, can I release my insistence on controlling results and trust God to be with me, one turn in life after another?

Holy Action: Today, stay alert to situations you feel compelled to control. Do you catch yourself procrastinating when you can't absolutely predict results? Don't berate yourself. Just *notice*. Then ask the Holy Spirit to use you, even despite yourself, and to help you believe that the *fruits* of the Spirit will come if you release the outcome to God.

Curiosity

Albert Einstein once said: "The important thing is not to stop questioning. Curiosity has its own reason for existence. Never lose your *holy* curiosity." Years ago I asked friends: "If you could choose the single most important quality for living life well, what quality would it be?" Such varied replies! Love. Perseverance. Sense of humor. Integrity. I said, "Curiosity." I never thought to couple it with the word "holy," yet isn't the capacity to wonder and to show curiosity, to welcome what is new, to keep our minds open to truth when and where we find it—isn't that another name for God?

Holy Action: What truth do you need to face up to in your life? Does your marriage need work? Are you still smoking or putting off an exercise program? Are you hurting those you love with your explosive words of anger? Are you ignoring your own ethical standards in order to hold on to a job? Prayerfully ask for grace to see one small step you can take in the next thirty days to respond to the truth you now acknowledge.

Doing All Right

Years ago, Kansas City minister Bill Hage remarked that everyone is born with a God-shaped vacuum inside. Since nature abhors a vacuum, we look for ways to fill it. Some people use money, expensive cars, big houses, powerful titles. Others cling to the wrong relationship, making someone else responsible for their happiness. But since the emptiness inside us is God-shaped, nothing but God can fill it. For years, I tried filling my emptiness with "rights"—associating with the *right* people, having the *right* possessions, pursuing the *right* career. I became a bona fide DAR ("Doing All Right"), only it wasn't enough. About ten years ago, I started meeting regularly with other DARs. We were seekers, and as we talked and prayed together, something shifted inside me, as if a peg's sharp, square edges had softened to fit a round hole. I went from being a DAR to a COG (a Child of God), recognizing, finally, that all I need to feel "right" is a right relationship with the Infinite.

Holy Action: Ask yourself these three questions: 1) Do you feel an emptiness inside, despite your achievements and possessions? 2) What are you throwing into the empty hole? Your job? Your family? Investments? Alcohol? 3) What must you do to invite God in?

Dreams

Karen is a fifty-five-year-old surgical nurse who dreamed for years of living in Colorado. But she earned a good salary in the Midwest and felt obligated to remain near her widowed mother, who lived in a Kansas City suburb. Then her mother died. Eight months later, on a visit to Leadville, Colorado, Karen saw a "For Sale" sign on a small mountain bungalow. When she went inside, she felt a powerful sense of "This is it!" She didn't know what the house cost, or if she could support herself in a town of 3,000, yet suddenly, said Karen, "Those were just details." Intuitively, she knew her life's dream was at hand. When her offer on the house was accepted, she quit her job, and with no clear picture of the future but a strong belief in her dream, she moved to the mountains where today she lives happily though frugally. We glimpse God's will for us through our life's dreams. Do I have the courage to claim my dreams?

Holy Action: What would you do if you absolutely, positively knew you could not fail? Write down your answer. In your answer lies the seed of your life's dream. Rewrite your dream as a goal, and break down your goal into steps until you find a step small enough to pursue. Are you willing to take that step? If not, meditate on what is stopping you.

Dysfunction

I laughed aloud when I read this paragraph in *The Forest Letter*, a newsletter from the Shantivanam retreat center.

"Isaac, though a God-fearing and devout man, was a co-dependent, an ACAF (Adult Child of an Abusive Father). He had recurring dreams of that day when his father tied him up on a makeshift stone altar and was about to plunge a large knife into his chest. Isaac also carried an intense, unconscious anger toward his mother Sarah for her part in it all. He never forgave her for not attempting to stop his father Abraham. Sarah knew what was going on, yet by her silence and refusal to act she was also a guilty party to his abuse. As a result, he distrusted most women."

What a modern way to read a Bible story! Aren't most families dysfunctional in one way or another? Looking back I see clearly my own parenting mistakes, and the psychological games our family played. Yet my children have grown into caring, functional adults who appear willing to forgive me for my imperfect parenting. Holy grace is surely at work when children offer absolution to their parents, yet it's only when we forgive our parents for not being God (and therefore perfect) that we reclaim them as human beings. It's also when we claim our own selves.

Holy Action: Ask yourself if you're still holding on to an unhealed hurt from childhood. *The Forest Letter* recommends: "Instead of hanging on to a painful injury, simply hand it back to the one who caused it. Use a sacred gesture. For instance, kiss the palm of your hand and gesture with your hand toward the other." You may need to hand back your wounds more than once. But as you persevere, you will find it gets easier and easier to release and let go.

Encounters

There is a gift in simply being present with someone, even if the encounter lasts only thirty seconds. When I make eye contact with the supermarket clerk or the gas station attendant or the person I collide with as I rush into an elevator, my eyes say to them, "I see you. You are not a *thing* to me. You are not an appendage to the cash register. You are a person." It is false humility to assume we do not make a difference. Today, I pray to make all my encounters count, even the ones that are thirty seconds long.

Holy Action: As you rush through your day, stay conscious of each interaction. Remind yourself that everyone you meet is a God-holder, and honor each person with eye contact and a smile. It doesn't matter if the person smiles back. You are offering a gift, not making a trade.

Endings

When my twenty-year marriage ended, I felt as profoundly shattered as my grandmother's vase, the one with the hairline cracks in it. It looked whole, yet one day, as I watched, it quietly broke apart into so many pieces. Yet in those shattered pieces, I discovered parts of me that I'd kept hidden—even from myself. What shattered, I realize now, was my ego: the public persona I'd clung to all my life. What has emerged is a more authentic me. It is never easy to pick up the pieces, yet sometimes it takes a shattering to humble us enough to let God's grace work in us.

Holy Action: Another name for *ending* is *beginning*. Think about an ending in your life—a job, a relationship, a domicile. For five minutes, write without stopping and express what pained you about the ending as well as what new beginning it led to. Can you see in the process the action of God's grace?

Enemies

Richard Rohr, a Franciscan priest and expert on the Enneagram, an ancient tool to help us understand our inner selves, says that in the spiritual life, enemies are your best friends. "[It's] why Jesus says, 'You must love your enemies.' For until you let the enemy in, you'll never face your dark side." During our divorce, my ex-spouse and I acted like enemies as we wrangled via our lawyers. *How can I ever love this intimate enemy?* I wondered. Not as I loved my marriage partner, but with an *agape* love for the messenger who helped me grow by forcing me to look at my dark side even as he showed me his?

Holy Action: Often we project onto someone else the dark qualities in ourselves that we don't want to face. Think of someone you dislike and consider the qualities that you disapprove of. Can you see any of them reflected in yourself? Who do you know who would answer with compassionate honesty if you asked whether some vestige of these qualities appears in you?

Envy

Oh, how I once put halos around people. People who seemed to have it all prompted my envious gaze at their "perfect" lives. Bob Beamis, the executive vice president of the ad agency where I worked, was a particular icon. Bob had the blond good looks of a movie star; instinctively you knew he had never had a pimple as a teenager. Life flowed so easily for him; I wasn't surprised when he was tapped to be the agency's president. For years, whenever I hit a snag, I would compare myself to Bob and say, "He never has this kind of problem." Then one day headlines appeared: "Beamis Ousted from Ad Agency." A political coup had cost him his job in a humiliatingly public fashion. In Rabbi Harold Kushner's book *When Bad Things Happen to Good People*, he says, "Anguish and heartbreak may not be distributed very evenly around the world, but they are distributed very widely. If we knew the facts, we would very rarely find someone whose life was to be envied." How true. Real halos come not from living problem-free lives, but from a willingness to live for God in all situations.

Holy Action: Have you "haloed" someone? How can you gain a more well-rounded picture of that person? Read a biography of someone famous who appeared on the surface to have had it all. Think how *your* life might appear to someone who sees only your surface successes.

Ethics

Yesterday, I bumped a car's fender in a parking lot, and I wrestled with myself. Should I leave a note? It was such a small bump, and my car wasn't scratched, though it looked as if a dent *might* be in the other car. Was I responsible? Or was the dent already there? Finally, I realized I had to leave a note because if we try to live honestly, we do it always and in all ways, not just when someone sees us. I hope I didn't make the dent, and if I did, I sure hope it won't raise my insurance rates. But I'm glad I left a note.

Holy Action: We get in the habit of overlooking small ethical lapses. Do you take home supplies from work that properly belong to your employers? Did you ever fudge— just a little—on an expense report? If a sales clerk undercharged you, did you pocket the excess change? Do you ever tell a "white lie" to save face? Think about your small lapses, and next time one is about to occur, ask yourself if you want to make a different choice.

Exploring

Here's what my friend Edward Hays, a Catholic priest and a gifted writer, told me a few days before my fiftieth birthday: "The fifties can be our most creative decade, Barb. Why, it takes fifty years just to collect our material. But you must force yourself to rethink old patterns and be willing to strike out in new directions. Go beyond what is comfortable and known. Our fifties are a time to experiment, as all great artists do. And after all, aren't we all artists—cocreators with God—when it comes to our own lives? Even if the outcome is not what you expect, it can lead down an interesting road. Celebrate fifty and explore!"

Holy Action: Give yourself permission, at least twice a week, to read about, think on, or do something you've never found time to do before. Visit an art gallery on your lunch hour. Write a poem or start a family history as a gift to your kids. Start practicing photography or enroll in a class on sailing. As you begin your activity, offer your explorations as a holy gift to God.

Faith

My fingernails are the stubby kind, but every now and then, I splurge on a manicure. Yesterday, Lee, a beautiful Vietnamese woman, clipped and sanded them. She flashed a smile that Julia Roberts would have envied, and in halting English told me she had emigrated to California from Vietnam with her husband. He was an alcoholic and a compulsive gambler, so finally she divorced him and moved to the Midwest with her four sons. She fingered a medal of Our Lady of Perpetual Help and said, "My faith very important to me, so I send my sons to Catholic school where are values." Then she flashed another megawatt smile. "They good boys. Oldest is fourteen and have scholarship to Catholic high school, maybe college. I tell them, 'God always there for you, but you can't sit on your hands.'" As I laughed, she added, "Before my father arrange my marriage, I thought to be a nun, so is okay for me without husband. What I want most is to raise sons right. I pray always God help me." *What faith-filled strength!* I thought. That evening, I addressed an envelope to Lee and put in an unsigned note: "A gift for someone whose faith has moved mountains." When I dropped in twenty dollars, the Holy Spirit nudged. "Only twenty?" So I dropped in twenty more. God doesn't want us to sit on our hands—or on our wallets.

Holy Action: Have you encountered someone who has shown unusual faith in God and used that faith to overcome mountains? A great way to reinforce our own faith is to reward someone else's. And to do it as God's unknown messenger.

Fame

Yesterday, I glanced through *People* magazine while standing in the supermarket checkout line. *People* celebrates what French writer Chamfort called *the state of being known by those who don't know you.* In odd juxtaposition, I read one of Emily Dickinson's poems a few hours later. She wrote,

> *How dreary to be Somebody*
> *How public—like a Frog*
> *To tell your name—the livelong June—*
> *To an admiring Bog!*

Emily lived a quiet, hidden life in her father's house in Amherst, Massachusetts, and often described herself in her poems in miniature terms: as a daisy, a flower, a mouse, a little pilgrim. Few of her poems were published in her lifetime.

Thérèse of Lisieux, known as "The Little Flower," lived a hidden life also. She entered a cloistered Carmelite order of nuns and died at the age of twenty-four, though not before writing her autobiography. Published after her death, it led to her canonization as a Catholic saint. Like Dickinson, St. Thérèse spoke of herself in miniature terms. She desired, she said, to practice small acts of kindness and in this way to be a "little flower" in God's glorious bouquet.

People magazine would never have featured these nineteenth-century women. Their fame emerged after their deaths as people learned how they had quietly practiced their God-given gifts. Saints and artists don't look for celebrity. They live this premise: if we seek God's kingdom *first*, our light will shine when and where it counts.

Holy Action: Make a list of those people who have deeply impacted your life for good. Write a paragraph about each which describes how they helped you grow spiritually. Consider sending each of your personal celebrities a thank-you note.

Fear

For years, fear appeared in my mind like the glittering eyes of a wolf, circling me in the dark forest beyond my campfire, its eyes reflecting the flames and holding me in thrall. But my friend Don didn't believe in wolf's eyes. When he lay dying from cancer, he held his fear at bay with a simple technique. He gave it to God, as a child might. "Whenever fear tries to take hold," said Don, "I pretend I'm holding a yo-yo, and I yo-yo my fear back to God. Sometimes I have that yo-yo pumping twenty times a day, but God is always there to catch it." He grinned. "I'm becoming a real yo-yo champion." Don's mantra was, "*No fear yet.*" After he died, I put a Post-it on my computer that said in big letters: "No fear yet!" In my desk drawer I now keep a yo-yo, one with sparkles on it, and any time the wolf's eyes start to glitter, I pull out my yo-yo and pump.

Holy Action: Buy a yo-yo. Make it a holy symbol to remind you that God is always there for you, especially when you're afraid. But we must affirm our faith in God's presence by not giving in to the fear. Pump your yo-yo as many times as it takes.

Forgiveness

Oh God, I yearn to forgive, to release, to let go. Yet see me with fists clenched and resentment curdling inside like spoiled cottage cheese. I cannot let go of this issue on my own. My ego has freeze-framed the moment of hurt and pain, and blown it up like a malicious balloon in the Macy's Thanksgiving Day parade until it fills the screen of my memory. It is not my better self that clutches so, that feels the twist in the belly and the bile in the mouth. Beloved Father/Mother God, hear my plea. Touch my heart and help it to soften and melt in compassionate forgiveness, not only for the one who has hurt me, but for myself. Grant me the grace to see mirrored in the reflection of your great love for me a similar love for the person who has wounded me, and give me your eyes to see past the hurt. Gently, oh so gently, unclench my fists.

Holy Action: Remember that forgiveness is a process. You choose and choose again. Help the process by adopting these four steps of empathy training from the Institute for Healthcare Research: 1) Think about times you have hurt others. 2) Recall when you have been forgiven. 3) Visualize your aggressor's state of mind and explain the hurtful event from the aggressor's viewpoint. 4) Try to go beyond the event itself to feel the frailty and humanness of the person who hurt you.

Generations

Today I experienced the birth of my first grandson. In the hospital room, my son-in-law held out a white-wrapped bundle. "Meet Jacob," he announced, beaming. My daughter lay quiet, still tired from birth. Surely, I thought, it was only the day before yesterday when I was giving birth to her. Gently, I lifted Jacob from his father's arms. My breath caught. "You are the *child of my child*," I thought in wonder, and I saw the connection, mother-to-child, mother-to-child, extending forward and back through endless generations, like exquisite rosary beads. Each of us, I realized, exists as a prayer to God, and by our very existence, we offer praise.

Holy Action: Think about your own generational connections. Is there an older relative or a younger child who would appreciate your phone call or letter today?

Generosity

I am filled with a dizzying sensation of love. How loved I am by this crazy, irrational God of ours, who persists in loving me as I slip and slide through life. So often I ignore God. Or stamp my foot in a temper tantrum, wanting my *own* way. Yet God keeps loving me! Patiently, graciously, generously I am loved and healed and warmed by the incredible Divine light that never goes out. I give thanks for this gift of a mad, lunatic God. Can I do less than crazily, warmly love all those I meet?

Holy Action: Affirm aloud, "Nobody owes *me* anything, but I owe all good to all people." It's like giving up resentment in advance. No matter how the grocery clerk, your boss, or the driver in the car behind you behaves, you will choose a loving response today.

Gifts

My friend Susan watched in terror as her husband reached down for a newspaper and suddenly clutched his chest. "If Medivac hadn't reached us so fast, Jack would be dead," Susan told me later. Her eyes widened as she remembered the close call. Then she murmured, "I nearly lost my husband before I realized what a fine husband I had." As clearly as if she were standing beside me, I heard my grandmother's crumbly old-lady's voice: "You never miss the water until the well runs dry. Remember that, Barbara Helen." When I was ten, I thought she meant, "Drink more water." At fifty, I know better. How many times have I splashed and gulped the cold, clear water of my life and failed to taste the gifts that were running unnoticed through my fingers? A friendship I took for granted . . . a spouse . . . the everyday joys that come in jelly jars and daisies . . . and then—gone, like drops of water lifted to the sun, and I can't bring them back any more than I can reclaim the water drops. Today, let me reach out with conscious fingers to all that flows through my life and drink deeply of the ordinary blessings that I often ignore.

Holy Action: Find six blessings in the ordinary events of the past week. If a negative event comes into your life today, find a positive way to describe it. What is it teaching you?

Giving

I read that Mrs. Astor—the grand dame of New York society—was still, at ninety-six, personally supervising the dispersal of charitable funds through the John Jacob Astor Foundation. Yet she wasn't born to wealth. She grew up—as I did—in a military family and went through the pain of an early divorce, then the death of her much-loved second husband—all before she married into Astor wealth. And from all reports, she remained down-to-earth. I don't have the Astor millions, but aren't all of us called to give generously of whatever we do have? For some, it might be money; for others, an intangible, like a smile or a talent for empathetic listening. The question to ask is, "What do I have to give away?"

Holy Action: Be a conscious giver today. Send a check to someone you hear about who needs help. Do an unexpected kindness. Give your gift anonymously, remembering that, as it says in Matthew 6:4, "Your Father who sees what is done in secret will reward you."

Grace

When I worked as a writer for Hallmark Cards, I wrote this copy for the cover of a Christmas card:

> *In the crisp, clear darkness of a December night*
> *I look at the sky and ponder God . . .*
> *Creator of an infinity of stars*
> *Millions, billions . . . beyond any number I might count . . .*
> *Is it not a miracle, indeed, that God*
> *can look through the stars*
> *. . . to me?*

I was thirty-one when I wrote those words in response to a writer's assignment, and at the time, I didn't believe any of them. Painful life circumstances had shattered my comfortable, take-for-granted faith, and I felt adrift in an existential universe that had no particular meaning. When I looked up at the night sky, all I saw were stars. I didn't see God, nor did it seem as if God saw me. Yet twenty years later, I realize that even though it seemed as if God had abandoned me, it was God's grace that sustained and strengthened me during that anguished period. Gifts of the Spirit were all around me. While God does look through the stars to see me, sometimes I must look past my own doubts to see God.

Holy Action: Think of recent coincidences in your life. Psychologist Carl Jung coined the phrase "synchronicity" to refer to events that occur by apparent coincidence but actually are prompted by a higher force. Can you see the spiritual grace that may lie behind apparent coincidences in your life?

Happiness

While teaching at San Diego State University, I asked my freshmen students to write a theme on one of their life's goals. It startled me how many wrote, "My goal is to be happy." Is it a function of youth to think you find happiness the way you find your car keys, simply by looking? At midlife, I realize my happiest moments have sidled into my life on cat's feet. I remember a moment while camping in the Sierras when I sprawled on my back, half-hidden in the grass of a high mountain meadow, my face raised to the sun, listening to my small children laugh with their father at the edge of a stream. Another moment occurred years later as I walked between my two grown sons. I looked up at one, then the other, one six-foot-two and the other six-feet tall, both blond and handsome, each taking long, confident strides, and my heart swelled with happiness because they had made it! They were ready to face the world as adults, and I rejoiced! When we chase happiness directly it often eludes us. We have to let happiness find us—and then recognize it when it occurs.

Holy Action: Write down five of your happiest moments. Notice: Were they big occasions or small? Expected or unexpected? Long-lasting or fleeting? What has made you happy this past week? Can you choose to be happy no matter what happens? Observe your instinctive response to that question.

Health

Last Saturday, I went bicycling by myself, exploring the countryside beyond Kansas City. The air held a tang of autumn, trees were a riot of red and yellow, and I felt buoyed by my own good health. As I thanked God for my healthy body, and the ability to pedal forty miles, I remembered a definition I'd read about health. "Health is not merely the absence of disease or infirmity, but a state of general well-being." It reminded me of the *dis*-ease I'd felt before my marriage ended. Depression dogged me as I wrestled with an increasingly vituperative relationship. Surely it's no accident that fifty percent of the healings mentioned in the New Testament were healings of the spirit, for a failing spirit can hurt more than a failing body. Yet the path to healing often takes us through pain, and before I could reclaim emotional health, I had to accept the pain of marital separation. Now, three years later, as I pedaled joyfully past farm fields and rustic barns, my spirit sang along with the psalmist, "Praise the Lord, O my soul! Who heals your disease . . . redeems your life from the pit . . . Praise the Lord, O my soul."

Holy Action: Are you stuck in a situation that is causing painful *dis*-ease? Examine the fear that keeps you imprisoned. Are you choosing neurotic pain over legitimate pain? Legitimate pain takes us through and leads to healing; neurotic pain recycles what is familiar. For more assistance, read M. Scott Peck's book *The Road Less Traveled*.

Hope

My friend Howard teaches theater at a Midwest university, but he grew up in Australia ". . . where it's bleak and barren in the outback," he said. "There is poverty to the landscape. Yet in the midst of the bleakness, the most beautifully colored birds lift suddenly into the air, taking wing before you—as if God placed these richly plumaged birds as a sign of hope in the wilderness. We need to look for the winged colors of hope in our own personal deserts." Yes. Sometimes, on days when I feel harried and strung out, it's hard to see the winged colors of hope; or do they take flight so quickly, I fail to notice?

Holy Action: Today, look for hope's bright plumage, even if your life has lately been a desert. Remember that we are most likely to see what we open up our minds to see.

Hurt

Ever reread a painful letter and feel the hurt all over again? It happened to me last week when I came across an angry letter written by my ex-spouse. Yet after awhile, I thought: Isn't this silly? I'm allowing black squiggles on a piece of paper to fill me with negative energy. It isn't the writer who's doing it because he doesn't even know I'm rereading his letter. *I'm doing it to myself.* We can always choose how we respond to situations. My prayer this morning is to remember that. And not pay attention to old black squiggles.

Holy Action: Are you harboring hurt feelings? Peace Pilgrim, the woman who lived as a saint walking thousands of miles for peace, told others that all inner hurts are caused by one of three choices: our own wrong *actions*, our own wrong *reactions*, or our own wrong *inaction*. Identify which of those three is responsible for your hurt feelings. Take charge of releasing your hurt by changing your action, reaction, or inaction.

Identity

There's a Buddhist saying: "Show me your original face, the face you had before your parents were born." For some, that's a terrifying idea. The reason many people stop psychotherapy is their fear of discovering their "original face," assuming that their inner core will be ugly and evil. I spent two-thirds of my life hiding behind my public persona, the "me" I thought others expected me to be. But in her book, *The Hero Within*, psychologist Carol Pearson says, "If we do not risk, if we play prescribed social roles instead of taking our journeys, we experience a sense of alienation, an emptiness inside." At last, in my fifties, I am trusting who I am. It has required some counseling to build that trust, yet I discover with joy that as I display my original face, I meet others who have dared to show theirs.

Holy Action: To say *I am* is to acknowledge the God or Christ within, and self-discovery is a life-long process. What have you already done to find your original face? Honor yourself for that. Journal about the fears that may be holding you back from further self-discovery. Are there books, friends, tapes, classes, or personal counseling that could assist you in deepening your self-discovery? Make a commitment to explore them.

Instructions

As I drove through Philadelphia recently, I got lost and stopped for directions. "Piece of cake," said the clerk inside the Quik Shop. Uh-oh, I thought, because that's what the last man had said, five miles back. It's hard to give directions along a familiar route. Because *you* know it so well, it's easy to forget details the stranger doesn't know. I've noticed it's the same when someone goes through a major life crisis. "Just move on," say well-meaning friends, but they neglect to tell you *how*. How do you move beyond the grief, the anger, the sadness? Maybe it's best not to try to give instructions, but to hold a friend's hand and say, "I know you feel lost. Want to talk about it?"

Holy Action: Think about the last time a hurting friend or family member came to you. Did you quietly listen or immediately start giving advice? Resolve to offer no advice unless it is specifically asked for, and practice "active listening" instead. Pay close attention to a person's words and body language and echo back what you think is being said. This kind of listening allows another to verbalize his or her own answers.

Joy

I call bicycling "meditation in motion." There's such profligate joy in pedaling past yellow daffodils or smelling new-mown grass as my tires spin against asphalt. Like someone praying with beads, I pray with each turn of my wheels, feeling in total harmony with the natural world around me. "Lord have mercy . . . Christ have mercy . . . Lord have mercy . . ." In my car, I'm always trying to get somewhere fast; but on my bike, it's the journey that counts. Even when a pothole ripped off my bike's rear reflector light, I shrugged off my irritation. Aren't potholes simply part of the journey? Help me remember that even when I'm not on my bicycle.

Holy Action: What activity prompts in you a spontaneous feeling of *joy*? Skiing? Playing the piano? Cooking? Playing with grandchildren? Being with your beloved? No matter how busy you are, schedule into your calendar a regular expression of what gives you joy, that "something" you treasure for no reason other than the act of doing it.

Kindness

Last year my friend Bev started jogging at 6 a.m., when it's still dark in the winter. Her jog took her past a large construction site, and even so early, there were usually some construction workers out. One morning, a big, burly worker approached her. "Uh-oh," thought Bev. But with a grin, he held out an orange vest. "Lady, you're not safe, running in the dark the way you do. The guys and me, we got a little worried, so we bought you this." Talk about love in action! Today, O God, open my eyes to notice if someone is stumbling in the dark; help me show as much kindness as those construction workers showed to Bev.

Holy Action: Do something kind for someone who rubs you the wrong way or someone you don't especially like. Pay attention: How difficult is it to make yourself do it?

Learning

When my grandson Jake was learning to walk, I watched. He pulled himself up on the corner of a chair and stumbled forward until—*plop!*—down he fell on his well-padded rear. Jake looked surprised, but he didn't cry. He just pulled himself up again. After he fell three or four times, I chuckled, thinking to myself, "I wonder if Jake is saying in his baby mind, 'Well, that proves it. *I'll* never walk'?" Of course not. To Jake, falling is part of the learning process. It's a gentle reminder that God doesn't count the times we fall either. Help me to remember that, O Lord, next time I fall while taking steps along my own spiritual path.

Holy Action: Have you let a failure discourage you? Are you tempted to give up on something because you've experienced rejection? Redefine *failure*: it's not a judgment. It's merely market information telling you what doesn't work. What have you learned from the experience that will help in your next try? Nothing is ever lost.

Letting Go

In 1989, my friend Lois lay ill with cancerous melanoma. She tried to pray, but her mind stayed trapped in the fearful words, "I don't want to die." Then Hank, a close friend from church, brought her a papier-mâché clown attached to a parachute. "Here's your let-go-and-let-God clown," he said. Lois couldn't help it. She laughed, especially when Hank hung the clown on her I.V. pole, where she could watch him bounce up and down beneath his parachute. All through the next few hours, Lois looked at the clown with his silly smile and painted cheeks, and gradually peace replaced her fear. "I didn't so much claim life as claim a surrender to God," she said. "I knew I wanted to live, and hoped I would, but I let go of my need to control life's outcome." Several years later, Lois is alive and well, the cancer in total remission. What if the outcome had been otherwise? "I had let go," Lois murmurs.

Holy Action: What is hardest for you to release? Hurt that hides behind anger? A feeling of rejection? Shame? Generalized anxiety about the future? On a sheet of paper, write, "I am afraid to release my _____." Then explain what you think will happen if you let go. Write as long as the words flow. Read your words out loud. Do some of your fears sound irrational? Which fears sound legitimate? On a second sheet of paper, write for three minutes on how you can encourage yourself to release. If you feel stuck, pray for guidance and repeat this exercise tomorrow.

Love

My friend Laurie told me how, years ago, her husband experienced a peculiar brain disorder that left him unable to feel or express the emotion of love. Laurie kept right on loving him even though he lacked the capacity to show love for her. After nearly two years, he recovered. Was it due to medication—or to the power of her unconditional love? Laurie truly lived the St. Francis prayer—the part that says, "Help me *to* love, not to be loved." Today, I say that prayer in new humility, wondering if I could love as Laurie did.

Holy Action: Think about your close relationships. Have you unconsciously created a quid-pro-quo kind of love (I'll do for you, but only as long as you do for me)? For a week, do more for another than that person does for you, and notice how you feel about it. Resentful? Put upon? Pray the St. Francis prayer, concentrating on the last lines:

O Divine Master, grant that I may not so much seek
to be consoled . . . as to console;
to be understood . . . as to understand;
to be loved . . . as to love.
For it is in giving that we receive,
in pardoning that we are pardoned,
in dying that we are born to eternal life. Amen.

Memories

When my first husband died, unexpectedly and too young, I thought I would never leave grief behind. Eventually though, the memories were no longer colored in pain, and the children and I could smile as we said, "Remember when . . . ?" Now, thinking about my divorce from my second husband, I wonder if part of "divorce rage" comes because we feel robbed of our happy memories. A death can still leave a tender history; divorce leaves mementos of extinguished hope. It's the death of your dream of a lifelong commitment. When my friend Frank lost his position due to a company merger, he expressed similar outrage because he'd lost his dream of faithful service well-rewarded. In time, through prayer, can the amnesia of forgiveness erase enough pain to allow happy memories to stir?

Holy Action: For the next nine days, read aloud each day the twenty-third Psalm, substituting plural pronouns for singular while thinking of someone you want to forgive. Notice how you feel as you read, "He leads us *both* beside still waters. He restores *both* our souls." Let it remind you that we are all connected in our humanity and that we walk together through the valley of the shadow of death.

Metaphor

On Friday, I walked in the park with my friend Barbara. We ran—splat!—into a large spider web. Barbara said, "God's plans for us are a lot like spider webs: beautifully fashioned until we blunder into them, ripping and tearing them because we failed to look. Isn't it wonderful that God, like his faithful creature the spider, is able to reweave the webs we destroy?" Only Barbara could find a spiritual metaphor in the yucky feeling of a spider web splattered across her face!

Holy Action: Is there an event or hurt in your life that you have blamed on God when actually it happened through human error? There's a universal law of cause-and-effect, so if you don't like an effect, trace back and examine the cause. Without casting blame or guilt, accurately assess responsibility. Have you given God a bum rap?

Mission

Dave worked for the federal government, and when I interviewed him for a magazine article, he confided that he didn't particularly like his job. But, he said, "In ten years I can retire. Then I'll find something I *really* like to do." "Like what?" I asked. He sighed, "I don't know."

In one of his parables, Jesus described a man who decided to tear down his barns and build bigger ones to store all his riches so that *someday* he could relax and take life easy. God responded, "You fool! This very night your life will be demanded of you." How peculiarly human for us to see our lives extending into some limitless horizon and to imagine that we can set aside our riches (and our dreams) with a guarantee that we'll have a chance to pursue them "later." *What if later never comes?* What if Dave is not alive in ten years? It's like the *New Yorker* cartoon whose punch line says, "I got married to avoid writing." How cleverly we find reasons to avoid pursuing what really matters to us. O Lord, help me find the courage to pursue my dreams *now.*

Holy Action: Meditate on what you really want to do in life, keeping in mind this image: a large, red American Beauty rose and a dainty purple violet. Which is more beautiful? Isn't each one lovely in its own way? It's not necessary to pursue your dream on a grand scale. Maybe you paint watercolors on the weekend. Or use your singing talent in a local civic chorus. Or enroll in one college class at night. The key is not to wait. Because *later* may never come.

Money

Twenty years ago, I worried a lot about money. Or rather, the lack of it. My husband was out of work, our family's financial future depended on me, and I felt burdened by the responsibility. "If I had more money, my worries would be over," I complained to my friend Don. He raised an eyebrow. "Don't put your faith in your bank balance, Barb. 'Where your treasure is, there your heart will be also.'" He showed me an interesting statistic. While personal consumption has doubled in forty years, the percentage of people satisfied with life remains the same—about thirty-three percent. If having more "things" doesn't guarantee more happiness, what does?

Don encouraged me to start tithing as a way to focus on all I do have, rather than what I don't have. He pointed to Proverbs 3:9 where King Solomon says, "Honor the Lord with your wealth, with the *first* fruits of all your crops. Then your barns will be filled to overflowing and your vats will brim over with new wine." I was scared when I wrote my first tithing check, but gradually, I've learned that it's true: "When you give, you receive, and your needs will be met." Just don't expect a direct payback.

Holy Action: Write a money autobiography. What were your happiest moments connected to money? Your saddest? Your scariest? Most people have no idea why they feel as they do about money. They don't understand the emotional content of money in their lives, or what messages they learned as children about saving, spending, and "having enough." Understanding your unconscious feelings toward money can help you deal with it on a more rational basis.

Motives

Lauraine is an insurance broker I know who won't take "no" for an answer. When Ted, a young man with a heart condition, came to her for help, he'd been turned down by three other insurance companies. But Lauraine kept making phone calls until she found him coverage. "I put so much time into it, I only netted $34," she told me. Her smile made it clear that earning money wasn't her motive. Jesus said, "Go not one mile but two." I wonder if I would be willing to go the extra mile for someone—even if it netted me just $34? I hope so.

Holy Action: Think about an occasion when someone went the extra mile for you. What did it cost the person in time, money, or effort? Were you sufficiently aware and grateful at the time? When did you last extend yourself for someone? How did your actions make you feel? Be alert today to any opportunity you have to go the extra mile. Notice if you choose to do it. Don't judge yourself. Just notice.

Natural Law

In the Midwest where I live, spring brings a riot of tulips and jonquils and daffodils, red and yellow and purple; giddy, joyful flags that proclaim, "New life! New life is here!" To get tulips in the spring, you plant bulbs in the fall. Though my friend Mary wasn't an experienced gardener, she bought three dozen bulbs, dug down in the dirt eight to ten inches, added potting soil, and then, to make sure she'd done everything right, double-checked with a gardener friend. Her friend immediately asked, "Did you plant the bulbs *face up*?" "Bulbs have faces?" blurted Mary. Like Mary, I never knew bulbs have faces. What if Mary hadn't talked to her gardener friend? She could have planted all her bulbs face down, and in the spring not a single tulip would have bloomed. Then Mary might have said, disappointment edging her voice, "Well, God didn't intend me to have tulips." But God had nothing to do with it. Natural laws have natural consequences. How many times—out of ignorance or because I haven't learned all I need to know—have I planted seeds the wrong way and then blamed my poor harvest on someone else . . . God, the government, a boss, my parents, or whatever higher power "out there" seemed easiest to finger?

Holy Action: Is there something in your life you don't like? When you dislike an effect, trace it to the cause, and you may find hidden in the cause a choice you made, even if your choice was unconscious. "As you sow, so shall you reap." Cause-and-effect, or *karma*, is a universal law. Without blaming yourself, observe what you may have done to contribute to what has occurred. Can you make another choice? If not, pray for the wisdom to accept what you cannot change.

Offering

Ask a teenage girl what she likes to do most and *shopping* will be near the top of the list. So when my fourteen-year-old niece Katie came to visit last summer, we headed for the mall. One of the stores had a big sign out front: "SALE! Buy one—Get one free," and Katie dragged me inside. "What a great sale!" she crowed. I smiled, thinking, God makes us the same offer. There it is in big letters. "Seek first the kingdom of God and all else will be given to you." What an incredible overture. To get my freebie, all I have to do is buy into God's kingdom. The kingdom isn't cheap, of course. In one of his parables, Jesus called it the pearl of great price. Yet what a generous merchandiser is God. Because even if I have to sell all I own—which means getting rid of all the baggage my ego carts around—as soon as I buy the pearl, I'm immediately rewarded. *All else is given to me*. Isn't that an offer I can't refuse?

Holy Action: Meditate on the question: If it is such a great offer, what holds you back from buying into the kingdom?

Openness

Mary Hines, Ph.D., is one of my buddies. She's also a Catholic theologian who talks and writes about *surrender*. To surrender, she says, stop clutching at life with clenched fists, and instead, let your hands fall open. Accept and rejoice in *all* events, believing that God's will is for our ultimate good. Her comments reminded me of my interview with Dr. Gerald Jampolsky, the physician and author of *Love Means Letting Go of Fear*. Dr. Jampolsky has hung a collection of photographs on his wall, each showing hands that are open. They remind him, he says, of what we must do if we want to receive love.

Holy Action: Today, notice: Are you are greeting life with open hands or clenched fists?

Orphans

A few days after my mother's death, I stood in the living room of the family home and sadly surveyed the treasures of my parents' forty-six years of marriage. Beside me, my brother Rob sighed, then murmured, "We're orphans, Barb. Adult orphans." It's one of the more poignant passages of midlife. Once both parents are gone, all kinds of other changes occur: sale of the family home, loss of a family center, dispersal of family treasures, and the discomfiting awareness: "I am now the oldest generation." And then— fleeting, terrible—another thought: "I'm the next to die." Yet I've learned a happy truth in the years since my mother died: our parents' spirits become integrated into our own psyches in a way no one else we lose ever does. We incorporate our parents as parts of ourselves, and when we're conscious of this, we can choose which aspects of them to hold on to and which to lovingly release. Even knowing that our lives no longer stretch out in an unending drift of years can be a blessing, for it may act as a catalyst to propel us into pursuing dreams we have set aside. Today, I thank God for the parents who gave me life; I honor their humanness, and I accept responsibility for my own life.

Holy Action: If your parents are alive, investigate your feelings: Are you carrying any grudges for mistakes they may have made in raising you? Do you accept them for who they are, acknowledging their strengths and weaknesses? Have you forgiven them for failing to meet all your childhood needs? If your parents are gone, release them lovingly. Forgive yourself as well as them for anything that didn't get resolved while they were with you.

Pain

Reflections after knee surgery: The pain and helplessness I felt when the cartilage tore in my knee helps me understand so much better the pain and fear that others feel who suffer a serious wound or illness. It's easy to dismiss another person's pain, or become impatient, even irritated, especially if the injury that causes the pain isn't visible, or if the pain occurs from a lifestyle choice. ("You have emphysema? Well, you were *warned* about smoking.") O Lord, thank you for the momentary gift of pain because it is teaching me what otherwise I might not know. Allow my pain to help me be more empathetic to the pain of others.

Holy Action: Think about a time when you experienced pain, either physical or emotional. What responses from others helped you tolerate the pain? Do you know someone who is experiencing pain now? Examine your feelings. Are you avoiding the person? Are you impatient or uncomfortable because you don't know what to do? Make a decision to lovingly visit a friend who is in pain, knowing that while you may not have the power to stop the pain, you do have the power to show compassion.

Paint Chips

A friend dropped by while I was painting a hallway and kept me company for a while. He told me about a paint tarpaulin he owns that holds in its creases tiny chips of colored paint that reflect his entire adult lifetime. "In those paint chips I see the history of twenty-five years," he said. "My first apartment after college, the living room of the house we rented when I married, our baby's nursery, the family room in the first house we bought. . . ." It's like a quilt, I thought, only he's saved scraps of colors instead of fabric. Everyone needs a way to save special memories—with photos or letters or quilt pieces or paint swatches. Like explorers who mark trees along an uncharted trail, my friend used paint chips to remind him of where he'd been. Out of our past, we learn *how* to go forward. We may paint over old colors by adding a new relationship, changing our lifestyle, or rearranging geography, but even then, the old colors aren't lost; they're only hidden. Every so often, we can shake out the tarpaulin, scratch through to old paint, and recall where we've been. And how we got from there to here, which may help us know the direction to go next.

Holy Action: Where do you keep the visible markers of your life? Memories need to be looked at now and then, for our ability to recall the past and contemplate the future is what sets us apart from lower animals. If some memories seem too painful, ask for the gift of holy amnesia, and let them go. Paint over your hurt with the bright colors of gratitude for where you are now.

Paradox

Joseph Campbell, the mythologist, coined the phrase, "Follow your bliss," by which he meant, dare to do what brings you joy. If you do this, you will be following God's will, for God's will for us is joy. Or bliss. But sometimes joy occurs beneath an outward appearance of pain. Sören Kierkegaard, the Christian existentialist, said faith means believing that only good comes from God, and the absurdity is that we must look for good even in apparent tragedy. Isn't that the paradox of Abraham and Isaac? Abraham, asked to sacrifice his son, willingly lifts the knife, while simultaneously believing that only good comes from God. Today, can I be Abraham? Can I bend in faith to all that comes into my life, believing that if I place God's will above my own, the absurd, wonderful truth is: I will find what is good? I will discover my bliss? God will tell me to set down the knife?

Holy Action: Are you following your bliss? If not, what stops you? Have you identified what brings you joy? Write for three minutes on the topic, "I feel joy when . . . " Write as fast as you can, with as little conscious thought as possible. Read what you have written. Are there any surprises?

Paying the Piper

This afternoon I took my small grandsons to a children's play about the Pied Piper of Hamlin. The piper made a deal with the villagers to rid their town of rats, but after he succeeded, the villagers refused to pay his fee. So the piper led away their children, something infinitely more precious to them than money. The play's message struck home with a powerful force. Many times I've deluded myself and ignored reality because I didn't want to "pay the piper." But I've always paid a bigger price later. A minister friend calls it "getting hit over the head with a cosmic two-by-four." Jesus put it this way: "Whoever wants to save his life will lose it, and whoever loses his life for me will save it." I pray for strength to face the truths in my life and for courage to pay the piper early, before I get hit with the cosmic two-by-four.

Holy Action: Get real. Do an honest self-examination; what the Twelve-Step program calls Step Four: make a searching and fearless moral inventory. Look at the excuses you have found for avoiding personal responsibility. Who are you blaming for the problems in your life? The key is not to blame anyone (including yourself), but to become accountable. With your hand reaching toward God, say aloud this affirmation: "I am responsible for my choices." It's another way of saying you're willing to pay the piper.

Perception

Sitting in my office, I'll sometimes hear a train whistle, stretching back into space like a long string of *Ooo's*. The rumbly sound of wheels along the track is a sound yet not a sound, almost like a rhythm inside me, the way one feels the rhythm of a heartbeat. Sometimes the rhythm is a lonely one; at other times, it's an exciting call, beckoning me farther along the journey. The train whistle sounds no different either way; it is my perception—whether I'm hearing it from fear or faith—that gives the whistle its particular meaning.

Holy Action: Today, become a watchful observer of yourself, and if an experience appears negative, consider how to *reframe* it more positively. Notice if you resist reframing. Psychological research shows we sometimes hold on to negative perceptions, even when we know they're not good for us, because the negative is familiar and, therefore, seems more comfortable. Before we can change, we first have to see. So *watch* yourself. It's a word that appears frequently in scripture.

Persevering

Occasionally I bicycle with Susan Clymer, a successful children's author. "I have a good imagination, but my writing skills aren't exceptional," she said as we pedaled along. "I simply work at it." Her comment reminded me of Woody Allen's quote, "Ninety-eight percent of life is simply showing up." God gives unique gifts to each of us and asks only that we fully use what we are given. But that means showing up and doing the work. Sometimes I wish I could be anywhere else besides sitting at my computer, typing words onto the screen. But I've discovered that if I'll just stick to it, the end results are the same, whether the *act* of writing is easy or hard. The same is true for meditation. I've learned that if I sit in dedicated silence, even though I'd rather be somewhere else, my spirit eventually grows quiet.

Holy Action: Visualize an experience in which you felt totally engaged and successful. What were the functional elements of that experience? How can you replicate them to achieve new goals that matter to you?

Potty Prayer

Ever laughed so hard you lost a little brake fluid? It's more likely to happen in midlife, isn't it? Instead of sleeping through the night, now I get up once or twice, and I've learned that "nature's urges" translate into action faster than they used to. Yet, what is urine but holy water, a visible sign of the complex wonder of the human body, so beautifully designed to absorb nutrients and expel waste? My father said every bathroom should contain a dictionary. "It's a great place to sit and learn one new word a day," he said. But isn't the bathroom an equally good place for God's word? Nature's urge can remind me to say a prayer of thanksgiving for my healthy body. Those who are tethered to dialysis machines or waiting for a kidney transplant understand what a gift we have in this mundane function we take for granted.

Holy Action: Spend three minutes in conscious awareness of your body. Listen to your heart beat. Feel the pulse in your wrist. Curl your toes. Pick up an object and appreciate having an opposable thumb. Take a deep breath. Blink your eyes. Now say, "Thanks."

Prayer-in-Action

My friend Don reminded me, "When you feel lost in a void, don't pray for yourself, Barbara. Pray for someone else." And when we pray for someone, he added, we should also *do* something for that person. Pick up the telephone. Write a letter. Invite her to lunch. Suggest a walk. Listen. Call it prayer-in-action. Mental health experts tell us the same thing: when you're feeling down, one of the quickest ways to feel better is to do something kind for someone else.

Holy Action: Think about someone you know who could benefit from an act of kindness. Put your thought into action. Do it now.

Praying

Reaching life's midpoint makes you stop to count your blessings. One of my greatest blessings was my friendship with Don Campbell, who died five years ago. Tall, lantern-jawed, and twenty-five years older than I, Don wrapped his saintliness beneath a warm, inviting cloak of humor and humility. On my fortieth birthday, he encouraged me to set aside *an hour* each morning to pray. "I don't have time," I protested. "If you're serious about building a relationship with God," said Don, "you'll spend enough time with God to show you're serious." Well, I thought, wouldn't I find time to spend an hour with the U.S. President if I were invited? So why not an hour with Our Father/Mother God?

Holy Action: For one week, expand your morning prayer-time to sixty minutes, even if you have to get up an hour earlier. Include reading, meditating, and writing in a journal. The point is not to commit yourself long-term to an hour of daily prayer, but rather, to experience what it feels like when you do it.

Progress

When my perfectionist tendencies caused me to worry aloud about how far I had progressed on the spiritual path, my friend, Sister Marie, said, "Relax, Barbara. Don't judge yourself or measure spiritual progress. God will judge, and you don't know by what standards. All you know for sure is that God rejoices in your trying." Such a good reminder that it's not for me to decide how far I've come in my journey. Learning to live in grace doesn't happen overnight, but so what? God's time isn't our time. What counts is that I am serious about doing the work. If I continue in the process, it will lead to progress.

Holy Action: Today, in everything you do, focus on doing your best, but without insisting that it be *the* best. Do not compare your efforts to anyone else's. Just do the work and leave the rest to God.

Reality

In the room full of well-preserved midlife women, my former college roommate Shar was an anomaly. The rest of us, who had pledged the same sorority twenty-five years earlier, were carefully coifed, our faces smoothed with skin emollients and subtle makeup. Shar wore no makeup, and her face, like a well-worn leather purse, showed soft wrinkles around the eyes and mouth. Her long hair, streaked with gray, was parted in the middle and clamped severely around her face, giving her the look of an 1890s brown-inked daguerreotype. Shar and her husband Arch had centered their lives around simple, natural living with a focus on God. They eschewed materialistic "musts" like television and cosmetics. I saw in Shar's eyes the same good humor I remembered from college, but there was also a profound knowingness—as if in giving up worldly accruements, she had found the real world. And of all the women in the room, she seemed the most beautiful.

Holy Action: For one week, keep track of your television viewing habits. How many hours a day do you spend in front of the TV? The following week, give up television and use the time for spiritual activities, whether it is meditation, reading, or doing a kindness for someone else. Notice what it feels like to substitute spiritual work for TV. Are you comfortable or uncomfortable? How much do you miss TV?

Receiving

Margery Vogel was a large, soft woman in her mid-fifties, a Jewish mother in the best sense of the word, always reaching out to help someone else. When her breast cancer metastasized, it marched into her bones like the Philistines into Israel, until doctors sadly shook their heads, and her husband brought her home to spend her final days. He couldn't afford to quit his job—they needed his health insurance—so when he had to leave town overnight on business, I joined two other friends in Marge's bedroom to learn how to strap her into a medical corset that relieved some of her pain. Margery, the matriarch to whom others went for help, now lay naked, her soft body open to our clumsy fingers as we awkwardly pushed and shoved flesh into the corset. I felt embarrassed for her. Such a loss of dignity! When she winced, I mumbled, "I'm sorry," and it wasn't only for the pain I'd caused, but for the whole experience.

Then—was I hearing right?—Margery chuckled. "Isn't this the pits?" she said. The three of us, her friends, looked at one another. And suddenly, we all began laughing, giggling like schoolgirls, because it was that or weep inconsolably, and only now do I see the utter graciousness with which Margery rescued us from our embarrassment. Her laughter gave us a vibrant gift, for in it, I learned what it means to receive.

Holy Action: Let someone give you a gift—of time, effort, or substance—and observe how you respond. Do you feel an immediate pull to "even the scales" by returning a gift? Allow yourself to receive something without giving anything back but a warm, heartfelt "Thank you." Observe how easy or difficult it is to receive. Identify your feelings. Do you feel vulnerable? Lesser than? As if you're imposing? Losing power?

Rejection

Rejections are no fun, but Larry, who's in sales, said, "Barb, if you were suddenly promised that everything you marketed would be accepted, you'd be terribly bored. Without some rejection, there's no challenge." Maybe Larry's right: we appreciate life by embracing opposites. Sad versus happy, old versus young, short versus long . . . and acceptance versus rejection. In the past, I've coupled rejection with feelings of failure, but isn't rejection simply information? It's not a statement of good or bad. Help me remember that the next time an editor turns down one of my manuscripts. How can I appreciate the joy of acceptance if I never get rejected?

Holy Action: Look at rejection in these four ways:

Rejection is an opportunity to build my sense of humor.

Rejection is merely new information.

Rejection is a numbers game (every nine rejections yields one acceptance).

Rejection can lead to resurrection, if we practice Christian forgiveness.

Remembering

In the first bleak moments after my marriage died, the person who offered me the greatest support was my friend Indira. Now doctors have told her she is dying. Though not yet fifty, cancer has spread inside her, into her bones, until her body throbs with pain. She has not given up life, she says, but it is as if she has awakened. "I am remembering what we forget when we are born, Barbara; that this earthly life is but a dream, and beyond the dream lies the timeless Now. Soon I will step through the door"—I am surprised at how peaceful she sounds—"and go where I was before I was born."

Holy Action: Look around you. Say to yourself, "This chair . . . this computer . . . this notebook . . . none of what I see is real." For the next hour, see each thing—each person—as part of the dream we call life. Think about the moment you will awaken from the dream. Will you awaken as if from a nightmare? Or will your dream leave a satisfying sense of a life well-lived?

Repentance

Ella McCall's mantra is, "Love ya, baby!" I interviewed Ella for an article about one of Washington, D.C.'s largest homeless shelters. Ella, a large, compassionate social worker, understands the homeless in a special way because she's been there. She never went to high school, and at age fourteen, gave birth to the first of eight babies. Once she rode subways all night with two of her children because she had no place to live. She's been raped and physically abused. Who would have imagined that she would earn a bachelor's degree in criminal justice, a master's degree in social work, be honored by Catholic University for her outstanding achievements, and receive the Mayor's Citation for Excellence?

As I struggled to understand Ella's changed life, I read what English theologian Harry Williams said about repentance. It's not the mumbled word "Sorry." True repentance means a change of heart and mind; it involves living one's life on a new basis and in a different atmosphere. It is to die to what one has so far been and to be raised up to a new quality of life, and it usually emerges from chaos and confusion. Surely Ella McCall was raised up, and in return has raised up others. As I pondered this idea of repentance, another thought occurred to me. Isn't repentance the outcome of successful psychotherapy?

Holy Action: Using Harry Williams' definition of repentance, when and in what ways have you chosen to live on a new basis, in a different atmosphere? Was your life in chaos before that? Is it only now, looking back, that you see the evolving grace that led you into a new life? Is repentance affecting you now?

Resentment

I lay in bed listening to the faucet drip. I'd been asleep until the slow trickle of water, a sound out of sync with the customary night quiet, had penetrated my dreams. *Drip. Drip. Drip.* It was winter and cold, and I didn't want to get up. Sleepily, I thought, I'll ignore it. But the dribble of water seemed to swell, grow louder. Random thoughts flickered in counterpoint. I recalled the Buddhist saying, "Drop by drop the bucket fills up." Drop by drop, my ex-spouse and I had filled our buckets to the brim with corrosive resentments. I had mine, he had his, and each blamed the other. Drop by drop the corrosion rusted out the love that had brought us together. In our voices dripped the rancor of frustrated expectations, *"You're not who I thought you were. . . ." "Why can't you change . . . ?"* until the bucket spilled and the marriage washed away, leaving behind the dirty sludge of resentment. In the chilly darkness, I sighed, then pushed back the covers. Apparently, the faucet wasn't going to quit dripping on its own. Resentments don't quit on their own, either. It takes effort to turn them off. And sometimes we need the gift of grace.

Holy Action: Can you hear any drip of discontent in your relationships? How is it manifesting itself? Through angry words? Silence? Distancing? Whose discontent is it? Are you blaming another for the situation? Has resentment blinded you to the good that is in the other person? Keep a daily log for one week and write down something positive about the person who creates resentment in you. Notice if it changes your perspective.

Re-tiring

Don Campbell learned, a year before his sixty-fifth birthday, that he was ineligible for retirement benefits from the company where he had worked for eighteen years. So while Don's contemporaries were sliding into comfortable pensions, Don faced an uncertain future as an independent creative consultant. The unfairness of his situation would have embittered many people, but Don merely smiled his lop-sided grin. "With God's help, I can still *re-tire*," he said, and pointed to himself. "I'll put some new tires on this old jalopy and start traveling a different road, that's all."

Holy Action: Has life handed you an unexpected shift in direction? Like Don, look at it as an opportunity to *re-tire*. What do you need to learn, what support system should you develop, and how can you tap into a positive attitude so you can make good time along your new road?

Rewards

The movie *Nixon* opened with a quote from the gospel of Matthew: "What does it profit a man if he gains the whole world and loses his own soul?" President Nixon appeared to have gained the world, but success couldn't quiet his inner demons until ultimately they brought him down. My friend Don liked to say, "Stay alert to what god you serve. Is it the god of success? Fame? Fortune? Power? If you're a faithful priest to your god, you'll be rewarded in kind." Ah . . . *in kind*. I may win the success, fame, or fortune I crave, but will I have sacrificed my soul to acquire it? It has always taken courage to seek the one true God. Twelfth-century mystic Meister Eckhart understood this and offered the perfect prayer when he said: "Pray God to let go of god."

Holy Action: What false gods attract you? To find out, look at how you spend your time and where you put your energy. When you have identified your false god (and we all have at least one), say as part of your daily prayer: "I pray God to let go of god."

Rightness

My friend Ed, a human resources manager, said, "Here are four magic words that can lower the decibel-level in any heated discussion: *'You may be right.'* It's a great phrase because you're not saying, *you are right*, only acknowledging that *you may be right*." Why is it so hard to release our need to be right? I'm reminded of a cartoon caption: "Don't confuse me with facts; my mind is made up." Yet isn't the essence of empathy our willingness to acknowledge, now and then, "You may be right"?

Holy Action: Look for a valid occasion to use this expression at work or at home. Observe the response you get.

Rosetta Stone

For centuries, the meaning of key Egyptian hieroglyphics was lost to antiquity. Then, in 1822, archaeologists unearthed a stone with the missing translations chiseled on it, and Champollion, a Frenchman, decoded the mysterious into the understandable. God's will once seemed as hidden to me as those Egyptian hieroglyphics. When life presented choices, I would agonize, "What does God want me to do?" My friend Don pointed out that I had my own Rosetta Stone in the life and teachings of Jesus Christ. If I followed his way, I could be assured I was following God's will. Such a profoundly simple answer! Christians and non-Christians alike acknowledge the extraordinary wisdom of Christ's teachings. Yet simple is not the same as easy. It's harder to live Christ's teachings than to read about them.

Holy Action: Read Matthew, chapter 5—"The Sermon on the Mount." Can you follow Christ's instructions, just for one day? Notice which part of his sermon sets up some resistance in you. Make a commitment to work on that area.

Sacramental

When Laura's companion of six years ended their relationship, she was overwhelmed by loss. Laura was in the middle of a tough graduate school program that she hoped would lead into an entirely new career at the age of fifty-two. "But after Dan left," she told me later, "I couldn't sleep or eat or think. My house seemed crowded with reminders: a fat ceramic pig he'd brought me from Mexico. Silver earrings. Photographs." Unable to concentrate, she skipped so many classes, one of her professors issued a warning. Laura knew she had to cope with her grief if she hoped to stay in graduate school, so she created a ritual. She wrote Dan a farewell letter, gathered up everything he had ever given her, and carried it all to a big, metal dumpster. There she lit two candles, prayed for the strength to let go, and threw everything into the trash. "I did it sacramentally," said Laura. *A sacramental dumpster?* Yet—why not? A sacrament is a visible sign that confers an inward grace, and isn't that what Laura prayed for? The grace to find within herself the power to recover? Her trip to the dumpster didn't eradicate her pain, but the ritual gave her energy to go on; and six months later, Laura earned her degree. She's already been offered a job.

Holy Action: Is there someone you haven't forgiven or some situation that has left you in pain? Plan a healing ritual using candles, incense, prayers, or holy water. Release balloons into the sky. Plant a tree. Write out your pain or grievance and ritualistically burn the paper. Sprinkle the ashes to the wind. Or visit your own sacramental dumpster.

Saintliness

Poet Phylis McGinley writes in her book, *Saint Watching* (which she says is somewhat like bird watching), that what ties all saints together is the decision they make to follow God's word literally. I've always wanted to be more saintly. What if I accept Christ's message, not as flowery words said two thousand years ago, but as specific directions for successful living today? What would happen if I tried, for just one day, to *literally* live God's word?

Holy Action: Read the Gospel of Matthew and select just one message from Jesus. Now try to practice that message for one twenty-four-hour period. Notice when and where it becomes difficult "or seemingly impossible" to follow. What does this tell you about yourself?

Security

When I was growing up, my grandparents' house symbolized security to me. Inside their big old Victorian home, a cluster of purple, china tulips sat in precisely the same place on the hallway table year after year. Other things might change, but never those tulips, and that was immensely comforting to me. Once upon a time, we thought about our jobs the way I thought about those purple tulips. You could count on them being there, year after year. But not any more! Where do we go when the purple china tulips disappear from our lives? Perhaps our mistake is in placing our security in manufactured things, whether tulips or jobs. God creates the real thing, and real tulips don't disappear—they go dormant and bloom again. In uncertain times, it's good to remember that we're the real thing too. All we have to do is nourish our own inner bulb of faith.

Holy Action: Make a list of six ways you can nourish yourself. Ask yourself, "Who are the friends I can trust to nurture me?" And pray that God will nourish your inner bulb of faith.

Seeking

The phone rang at 11:15 p.m. Startled, I picked it up and heard my father's voice. At such a late hour, I felt instant trepidation. "Is everything okay?" I quavered. His chuckle touched me like warm molasses. "Can't I simply call my one and only daughter to tell her I love her?" He was sitting alone in his den, he said, reading. "Reading what?" I asked. "The Bible." Now I was really surprised. My father? The non-church-goer? "Why, Daddy, how wonderful!" I exclaimed. "Are you looking for God?" His chuckle embraced me. "Barbara, what makes you think I ever lost him?"

Holy Action: Think of the people you know who live God's word day to day. How many are regular church-goers? Do you know anyone who seems to be a "Sunday Christian," someone who goes to church on Sunday but forgets the message on Monday? Look for God-holders in unexpected places. You'll recognize them by their acts of kindness and compassionate smiles. They may or may not read the Bible.

Self-Fulfilling Prophecies

A friend has revealed a haunting secret. For most of her married life, her husband has accused her, over and over, of being unfaithful. "Barbara, I have *never* been unfaithful," she said, tears welling, "but his accusations hurt so much, I'm beginning to wonder if I should leave him." I listened, astounded. My friend is a woman of natural beauty and elegance, rather like Audrey Hepburn. She carries herself with similar grace and, like the actress, is known for her work with the poor and needy. She revealed her secret in a moment of desperation. I knew some of her husband's history: how his parents had abandoned him as a child, how he grew up in a series of foster homes, how he made his own way in life. Did some deep-seated sense of unworthiness prevent him from trusting in the love of his beautiful wife? Would his unfair accusations cause her to leave him, the very thing he feared most? O Lord, alert me to my own self-fulfilling prophecies, where I let my fear create what I say I want to avoid.

Holy Action: Do you hold an optimistic or pessimistic vision of the future? Get in touch with your attitude toward life by pulling out a piece of paper, and with your nondominant hand (left for right-handed people), draw a picture that expresses how you feel about life. Let your unconscious direct your hand. When you have finished your picture, write a paragraph about what it tells you. Remember, in life we don't get what we deserve but what we *think* we deserve.

Soaring

At a creative conference, participants were asked to write a poem, attach it to a helium balloon, and send it aloft into the sky, to land who knows where? "We could have taken home our balloons (and our poems) and tied them to the bedpost, but in the end, the balloons would have shriveled and we'd have lost them anyway," said a friend who attended the conference. Then she added, "Isn't that our choice in life? To tie ourselves to bedposts or to soar into Mystery?" Yes! Give me the courage to soar—even when I don't know how or where I will land.

Holy Action*:* Take a risk. Do something out of the ordinary. Drive to work a different way, invite someone to lunch that you would like to know better, read a magazine that holds a political view different from yours. Offer up the experience to God, as a way of soaring, if just a little, into mystery.

Solitude

The Southwest desert has always lured me. The beauty of the distant mountains, the wide expanse of sky, the rugged desolation of the land. On a recent trip, I was enjoying the solitude until I drove into a desert town. A festival was underway, and the peaceful desert silence disappeared into the chaos we call human civilization. I saw RVs, campers, carnival rides—even camel races! The camel rides hooked me. I parked, and stepped out to watch as two camels lurched awkwardly down a makeshift racetrack. As I watched the camels run, kicking up dust and spitting green bile, I thought about my own daily camel race. "Can't pray today! Too much to do!" I cry, and off I run. Or lurch. Yet if Jesus and the Hebrew prophets before him felt a need to retreat to the desert to pray, don't I? Today, give me the grace to climb off my camel and find the blessed solitude that refills my soul.

Holy Action: What is your "camel race"? What seems so important that it gets in the way of your desire to sit in the silence? What must you do to create the quiet of the desert in the midst of life's daily chaos?

Strength

"Life is like an annual rainfall," said Don. "Sometimes a downpour hits us all at once; and sometimes, we experience drought. But on an annual basis most of us receive just the right amount of moisture." Help me to remember Don's words, especially when I feel overwhelmed with problems at work or at home. Let me believe in the divine forecast: that healing rain will come again even if dust seems to blow into my life, and that if a downpour threatens, it will not overwhelm me, but strengthen whatever in me needs to grow.

Holy Action: Are you facing some emotional turbulance? Just for today, accept every problem in the sure belief that you have the strength to handle it.

Success

Yesterday, I met my friend Penny for lunch. Penny is creative vice president of a large advertising agency and always on local lists of "successful women." But as we sipped café lattés, she mused, "What if my life is not about my business success, but only about how kind I am when no one else is watching?" I laughed. God has a quirky sense of humor. Or maybe we're the quirky ones, forever thinking it's material success that matters when what really counts are our acts of compassion when no one "important" is around to applaud. Today, help me remember what success really is.

Holy Action: Perform an act of random kindness today. Do it so that no one else knows you did it.

Suffering

In a "Hagar the Horrible" comic strip, one of the characters shakes his fist at the sky. "Why me?" he shouts. In the second panel, a voice calls down from the sky, "Why *not* you?" It's the lesson everyone must learn—that no one is spared suffering, but I tried to duck the lesson just as most people do. When I first read Jesus' words that "Anyone who does not take up his cross and follow after me is not worthy of me," I thought it meant that if I committed to Christ I was stuck with carrying a cross; whereas if I didn't commit, I might be spared the cross. Such naiveté! Crosses are always with us, and most are ones we build for ourselves out of choices we make. What Jesus offers is a chance to find a higher meaning in our suffering. Otherwise, we get into the endless cycle of neurotic pain, which has no meaning at all. It's taken me years to understand that the answer to the question, "Why me?" is "Why not me?"

Holy Action: Are you avoiding legitimate suffering because you haven't faced the truth about your marriage, your parenting, or your addiction to tobacco or alcohol? If the question makes you uncomfortable, the answer is probably "Yes." Ask God to lead you to truth, wherever truth takes you, and then open your eyes. Watch yourself in your relationships, and attempt to see what is really happening.

Surrender

Theology professor Mary Hines says surrender is simple. "Merely acknowledge, 'God is God, and I am *not* God.'" Ah. Don't I play God every time I try to rescue or fix another? And how about the way I try so hard to control my life? Just for today, can I acknowledge that I am not God? Can I surrender to God's will instead of my own, which means saying the great "Yes!" to whatever comes my way?

Holy Action: If you're tempted to fix someone's problem today, back off. If you start feeling frustrated because things aren't going the way you expected, take a deep breath. Count to three and quietly say, "God is God, and I am not God."

Thriving

Nora Ellen gardens enthusiastically. "I've noticed," she said, "that certain plants like to go their own way. My lilies of the valley nudged themselves right into my neighbor's yard." Nora let them go. "I decided to give them their independence," she said. I laughed, because isn't it the same for us? Some of us nudge our way into places and situations where we don't belong, and the Divine Gardener lets us go. Yet if we put down our roots in the garden in which we're planted, isn't that where we're most likely to thrive?

Holy Action: Are you picturing greener grass on the other side of your fence? Does someone else's job or love life or family look better than your own? Think of ten blessings that are blooming in your own garden.

Tithing

Henry Thomas is a wealthy businessman who tithes *more* than ten percent of his income. "I was born with an aptitude for giving," he said. "Just as some people have a natural flair for music or sports, I've always found it easy to give." He wasn't patting himself on the back; just commenting on a natural talent.

It's important to give back from our gifts. Some people tithe money; others tithe their time and talents. My friend Leslie is extraordinarily generous in her help to friends and neighbors. She sends casseroles to the house-bound elderly, offers child care to a mom who has to go into the hospital, is a confidential listener when someone hurts. Another friend remembers birthdays and special occasions. It's not merely that she remembers your birthday *on time*, but that her gift or card is so uniquely suited to you. A prominent Kansas City businessman I know liked to send letters commending people for something they'd achieved or expressing sympathy for a loss. He wrote thirty letters a week, often to people he didn't know but had read or heard about.

The key to tithing, said my friend Don, is to commit *first*. Don and his wife Sally started putting ten percent of their income in a tithing account. Once that money belonged to God, it became fun to spend it. "We'd hear about a young single mother struggling to make ends meet, and send her a surprise check to brighten her Christmas; or get a letter in the mail from Foster Parents, Inc., and adopt a Filipino child," said Don. I find it's easier to tithe money when I also tithe time. An hour for prayer is about ten percent of the time I spend awake.

Holy Action: Consider the question of tithing. Explore your feelings. Butterflies in the stomach? Queasiness? An instant "No way! I can't afford the money (or the time)"? Which is easier to think of tithing? Time? Or money? Could you start with half-a-tithe at five percent?

Tolerance

The son of my down-to-earth, red-haired neighbor recently got married. My neighbor likes her new daughter-in-law, but her sister Patty, who dotes on her nephew, does not. Patty grumped and stomped around at the wedding like a horse's you-know-what. Did her behavior stop the wedding? Of course not. It merely caused a rift between Patty and her nephew. How many times have I acted like Patty, grumping about someone else's choices as if I expected to change their minds merely by stomping my feet? Help me find tolerance for other people's preferences. A temper tantrum never changes anyone's mind.

Holy Action: Experts tell us, "You can't change anyone else, only yourself." ("Don't look at the speck in someone else's eye; look at the plank in your own," said Jesus.) So think about some changes you'd like to see in somebody else. Now think about some changes *you* might make that could lead to such changes in another. Are you willing to change?

Universality

I've observed there are only a handful of basic truths. They get repeated in slightly different ways, depending on the culture, historical epoch, religious doctrine, or spiritual master. But the truths remain elemental and universal, and it is our life's work to discover and practice them. Here's my list:

Love God, not idols. (Not so easy in a society that worships money.)

Do no harm. (Avoid little murders of the soul.)

Live truthfully. (Trust that reality is friendly.)

Love your neighbor as yourself. (Stop being a perfectionist!)

Practice non-detachment to people and things. (Give up designer-label clothing. Stop trying to run your grown-up kids' lives.)

Surrender to God's will. (And your bliss. Did you know they are one and the same?)

Wake up! (Pay attention to the moment. Stop regretting the past and yearning for the future.)

Holy Action: Which of those truths seems hardest for you to follow? Practice that one for one day, noticing when, where, and why it gives you the most trouble.

Ups-and-Downs

For years, a Peanuts comic strip hung behind my desk. In it, Lucy sits on a curb, looking woebegone. Charlie Brown comes along. "Cheer up, Lucy, life has its ups and downs." Lucy jumps up. "But why? Why doesn't life have ups and upper ups?" How I laughed when I saw that strip. "That's me," I told people, "I'm looking for the Land of Upper-Ups." It's taken me 'til now to realize that if all we had were "upper-ups," our lives would be as bland as plain yogurt. I've done some of my best growing during the down times. (Isn't that where we find the fruit in most yogurt? At the bottom?)

Holy Action: Instead of looking for a mythical land of upper-ups, pray the Psalm: "This is the day the Lord has made. Rejoice and be glad in all things." Then, *act* glad.

Values

Earl, a suburban bank president, was one of my favorite clients. I admired a ring he always wore, gold with a small diamond. "The diamond is from my mother's engagement ring," he explained. "My dad died young and we were stone cold poor in Wichita, Kansas. Periodically, Mom would take her diamond ring to Mr. Frisbein's pawn shop and pawn it for what she needed: $50 or $100. What she really got was a secured loan, because Mr. Frisbein never sold the family heirlooms people brought to him. It became our family responsibility for all four of us kids to help earn enough to retrieve Mom's ring. The next time we needed help, though, back it went to Mr. Frisbein." Earl paused. "I try to run my bank the way Mr. Frisbein ran his pawn shop."

Holy Action: Think of someone you know whose values you admire. How did you see those values at work? How can you adopt similar values in your life?

Viewpoint

While on one of my weekend spiritual retreats, I crossed a small stream in front of the chapel by jumping from one rock to another. After doing this several times, I noticed, downstream, a path and a bridge. Once I saw the path, I laughed out loud. "How did I miss it?" I wondered.

Isn't life like that? There in full view is some aspect of God in my life, yet I don't see; I keep struggling, jumping across rocks, getting my feet wet, and ignoring the bridge. Oh Lord, help me to notice the bridges you place in my life and to feel grateful as I cross them.

Holy Action: Today, pay attention to the small details. Ask yourself, especially if you're trying to solve a problem, "Is there something I'm missing? Something so obvious I've let it escape me?" Notice what you see at the corner of your eye. Be alert to serendipity, and keep your feet dry.

Visibility

As a middle-aged priest, Pope John XXIII wrote in his journal, "It is hard for me to think of a hidden life, neglected, perhaps despised by all, known to God alone. Yet until I succeed in doing such violence to my own likes and dislikes that this obscurity becomes not only indifferent, but welcome and enjoyable, I shall never do what God wants of me." Surely I must come to that same place in my own willingness to serve God. It is hard, especially for someone who likes being visible as much as I do, to think of serving in obscurity. Yet can I pray as John XXIII prayed? To do my job well whether or not anyone notices?

Holy Action: Examine your motives before you take any action today. C. S. Lewis said, "The greatest evil is to pursue good for the wrong reasons." Ask God to help you live and work from the right motives.

Weakness

Shortly before publication of my first book, *My Angry Son*, I worried aloud about the painful family revelations it contained. My Jesuit friend, Fr. Joe Freeman, replied, "Don't be afraid to let the book show people your weaknesses. It's not who you were then, but who you are now that counts. Remember St. Augustine's *Confessions*? He described himself as a youthful reprobate. It's the journey that you and your son made that will give other parents hope." The grief shown when Princess Diana died gave eloquent testimony to the way a celebrity's humanness, her very foibles, could endear her. "She is one of us," wept the crowd. "The people's princess." Whenever we find the courage to reveal our humanness, are we not giving testimony to what links us, one to the other? And in showing our individual ways of growing, don't we give hope to others? It is not where you start or where you end, but the *trying* that matters to God.

Holy Action: One of the best ways to affirm another person is by listening. Listen quietly and try to understand someone's underlying message, not just the factual content but the feelings. Any time we listen with care, it encourages others to share their reality.

Worry

Over lunch, I worried aloud to my friend Barbara. She shook her head and smiled. "Don't you know there are two times *not* to worry? Don't worry if the problem is one you can fix. Just go fix it. And don't worry if the problem is one you can't fix, because worrying won't change anything." I laughed, and wondered, how many times do I substitute worry for the harder task of fixing? Jesus put it another way: "Do not borrow anxiety for tomorrow."

Holy Action*:* This week, if you catch yourself feeling anxious, ask, "Is it something I can fix?" If the answer is yes, go fix it. If the answer is no, stop worrying.